T0158773

POETRY

If Only the Road Could Talk: Poetic Peregrinations in Africa, Asia, and Europe 2017
City without People: The Katrina Poems 2011
Random Blues 2011
Days 2007
Tender Moments: Love Poems 2006
Early Birds: Poems for Junior Secondary, (Book One, Book Two, Book Three) 2004
The Word Is An Egg 2000
Horses of Memory 1998
Seize the Day 1995
Midlife 1993
Waiting Laughters 1990
Songs of the Season 1990
Moonsongs 1988
The Eye of the Earth 1986
A Nib in the Pond 1986
Village Voices 1984
Songs of the Marketplace 1983
Pages from the Book of the Sun: New & Selected Poems (1983-2001) 2002
Selected Poems (1983-1991) 1992

DRAMA

Two Plays 2005
The State Visit 2002

ESSAYS

Thread in the Loom: Essays on African Literature and Culture 2002

PUBLIC DISCOURSE

Dialogue with My Country 2007

green:

SIGHS OF OUR AILING PLANET

Niyi Osundare

BLACK
WIDOW
PRESS
BOSTON

Black Widow Press is an imprint of Commonwealth Books, Inc., Boston, MA. Distributed to the trade by NBN (National Book Network) throughout North America, Canada, and the U.K. Black Widow Press and its logo are registered trademarks of Commonwealth Books, Inc.

Joseph S. Phillips and Susan J. Wood, Ph.D., Publishers
www.blackwidowpress.com

Cover design & text production: Geoff Munsterman
Author photograph: Paul Punzo

ISBN-13: 978-1-7371603-3-5

Printed in the United States of America

Ale ni nin a (The Earth owns us)
Ia ni l'ale   (We own the Earth)
Ira aye, giri giri ko ni l'ale (People of the world, do not trample the Earth)
Tee jeje; tee jeje (Step gently on it, gently, gently; step gently on it).
—Yoruba song

We do not inherit the Earth from our ancestors; we borrow it from our children.

—A Native American saying

The care of the Earth is our most ancient and most worthy, and after all, our most pleasing responsibility.

—Wendell Berry

The tree which moves some to tears of joy is in the eyes of others only a green thing that stands in the way. Some see nature all ridicule and deformity... and some scarce see nature at all. But to the eyes of the man of imagination, nature is imagination itself.

—William Blake

Anyone who hasn't been in the Chilean forest doesn't know the planet.
—Pablo Neruda

The biggest enemy we face is anthropocentrism. This is that common attitude that everything on this Earth was put here for [human] use.
—Eric Pianka

Today we are faced with a challenge that calls for a shift in our thinking, so that humanity stops threatening its life-support system. We are called to assist the Earth to heal her wounds and in the process heal our own—indeed, to embrace the whole creation in all its diversity, beauty and wonder. This will happen if we see the need to revive our sense of belonging to a larger family of life, with which we have shared our evolutionary process.

Today, over 50 years later, the stream has dried up, women walk long distances for water, which is not always clean, and children will never know what they have lost. The challenge is to restore the home of the tadpoles and give back to our children a world of beauty and wonder.
—Wangari Maathai,
founder of The Greenbelt Movement,
Nobel Peace Laureate

Waters are dying, forests are falling. A desert epidemic stalks a world where the rich and ruthless squander earth's wealth on the invention of increasingly accomplished weapons of death, while millions of people perish daily from avoidable hunger.

Tomorrow bids us tread softly, wisely, justly, lest we trample the eye of the EARTH.

—Preface to *The Eye of the Earth* (1986)

CONTENTS

I   GREEN   3

II HOLE IN THE SKY   7

III IGI DA! (THE TREE HAS FALLEN)

    Igi Da (Yoruba original)   13
    Igi Da (English translation)   15
    Amazon Burning   17
    Treetalk   25
    Deep Green   26

IV OUR DYING PLANET

    Once Upon a Planet   29
    Climate of Fear   30
    Malingering Mountain?   31
    Dying Lake   33
    The Desert Cometh   34
    Kaningo   35
    Venice Under Water   36
    Melody Unheard   37
    The Sky Ain't Blue   38
    We Glow in the Dark   39
    Head in the Sand   40
    Corpses That Never Count   42
    Cancer Alley   43
    Refugee Camp   45
    Act of God   46
    Eco-snaps   47

V REDEMPTION ARMY

    Remembering Ken Saro Wiwa   51
    For Greta Thunberg   52
    The Delta Sings Between the Tides   54
    For Ibiwari Ikiriko   55
    Invocation   56
    Many Stars, One Sky   58
    Eco-Hints   59

VI BOUNTY

    For World Food Day   63
    Oba L'Agbe (The Farmer is King)   64
    Song of Life (2)   65

Ode to the Pine Apple   66
The Water Melon of Hargeisa   68
String Bean   69
My Kitchen Is a Garden   70
Harvest   71

VII SEASONS

Warning   75
Harmattan   76
Fall Fellows   77
Yellow Yawn   78
Timid Season   79
Autumn in New Hampshire   80
Early Spring in City Park   82
Spirit of Spring   83
Quest-ions (3)   84
Night Wings   85
Polygamous Moon   86
The Moon Who Came to My Garden   87

VIII WIND, WATER, AND PUNCTUAL PETALS

Wind   91
The Rainmaker's Daughter   92
Dewdrop (1)   93
Dewdrops (2)   94
Water   95
River   97
The Lake Which forgot Its Clothes   98
A Paddle Made of Words   99
Lily   100
Magnolia (1)   101
Magnolia (2)   102
Gbarijo   103

IX GREEN RESOLVE

Wishes   107
Connected   108
Remember   109
Dare-do   110
Stubborn Hope   111
Embers   112
Homecoming   113
Still We Sing   114

Notes   117

ACKNOWLEDGMENTS

The following poems made their first appearance in the outlets gratefully acknowledged below:

Caliban: French Journal of English Studies, No. 61, 2019: "Head in the Sand", "Wishes", "Remembering Ken Saro Wiwa".

World Literature Today, University of Oklahoma, 2014: "Wishes", "Hole in the Sky".

ISLE (Interdisciplinary Studies in Literature and Environment), Volume 15-2, Summer 2008: "The Desert Cometh", "Dying Lake", "Lily".

Moving Worlds: A Journal of Transcultural Writing, Vol. 14, Number 2, 2014: "Head in the Sand", "Stubborn Hope".

Water Testaments: Anthology of Poems on Water and Water-Related Issues, 2008: "Water".

Magma 37, 2007: "Polygamous Moon".

The Northern New England Review, Vol. 28, 2006: "Autumn in New Hampshire".

Paris Lit. Up. Number 4, 2016: "Deep Green".

Maple Leaf Rag V: (An Anthology of Poetic Writings, New Orleans), 2014: "The Lake Which Forgot Its Clothes".

Silver Lining: An Anthology of Nigerian Literature (A Nigeria PEN publication), 2019: "Ode to the Pine Apple".

The Nation, Nigeria: "Greta", "Song of Life", "My Kitchen Is a Garden", "Venice Under Water".

I

GREEN

In different shades, in different shapes

GREEN

Green salutations
Green intonements

Green affirmations
Green denials

Green calculations
Green engagements

Green fabulations
Green conjectures

Green skies

Green mountains
Green echoes

Green murmurs
Green mirrors

Green sciences
Green infinities

Green masks
Green faces

Green clay

Green feathers
Green flairs

Green fires
Green ashes

Green grass
Green grace

Green gba
Green gbu

Green

Green aspirations
Green awakenings

Green migrations
Green arrivals

Green intimations
Green estrangements

Green germinations
Green efflorescence

Green oceans

Green silences
Green songs

Green sadnesses
Green amusements

Green drums
Green tonalities

Green memories
Green encores

Green dust

Green stones
Green en-grave-ings

Green showers
Green abundance

Green rainbows
Green enchantments

Green possibilities
Green awakenings

Planet

II

HOLE IN THE SKY

The grass's green laughter
Has yellowed into sickening groan

HOLE IN THE SKY

*(Choreo-poem. Preferably with musical accompaniment, the tempo
varying according to the mood and meaning of each section)*

Eco-Snaps

i

Koko gba   kokodi
Koko didi   kokodi[1]

'Tell my story',
 Said the Earth to me
'Oh, tell my story the way it is.
Don't sugarcoat its bile
Don't varnish its rust
Don't cover its scars with pretty words
Tell my pain the way it is
            The way it is
            The way the way   the way   it is
Tell my pain,   the way it is'

Koko gba   kokodi
Koko didi   kokodi

ii

The day the river caught fire
And the lake burnt like Devil's oil
The mountain coughed like a broken giant
The sky's eyes were red with grief . . .

Factories whose lethal spills provoked the plague
Lay fortressed behind the hills
Ayekooto[2] sighted their owners
On their way to the city bank

    Koko gba kokodi

iii

Ever heard fruits arguing between the leaves
Over which got the deepest dose
Of the pesticidal plague?

The poison killed the pest
And later buried the people

    Koko gba kokodi

iv

The thunder of the sea
Rattles the silence of the sky
Wailing whales wonder about their woes
The deeper the dolphin dives
The shallower its desired relief

    Koko gba kokodi

v

The desert marches towards the sea
The desert marches towards the sea

Fire in its eyes
Mayhem in every movement

The desert marches towards the sea

With camel-loads of broken skulls,
Roasting iroko[3] trees for lunch
The mahogany for early dinner.
Dandelions roar beneath its feet.
The elephant grass has lost its tusk
To the famished poacher from sandy regions

The desert marches towards the sea

Alas, the boundless rainforest of my youth
Has shrunk to a frightened eyebrow
On the forehead of the coast

    Koko gba kokodi

vi

The midday sun
Cannot see its face in the lake
The turquoise sea is yellow
From the poison of upland plants

The day they killed a tree
In the ancient forest
The chainsaw left a dirge
On the lips of the leaves

There is a bird in my heart
Craving for a perch on the absent tree.

    Koko gba kokodi

      vii

Seasons of omen
Seasons of omen:
One-legged frogs
Babies with missing arms
The grass's green laughter
Has yellowed into sickening groan
Vengeful droughts digest the fields

    Koko gba kokodi

      viii

A hole
A hole
A blazing hole
In the garment of the sky

Oven-hot summers
Winters blind with ice
The Arctic melts like butter
As rising oceans consume the land

Fog-fraught cities grope
Beneath their fuming factories
The rain falls, acid,
On frightened forests

The Earth we used to know
Is once upon a time

A hole
A hole
A blazing, blinding hole
In the garment of the sky

    Koko gba kokodi

       ix

Trumpet sounds in the horizon
Green intimations unfurl the wind
Healing needle to the hole in the sky
Earth's Redemption Army
Is gathering strength beyond the clouds.

Trumpet sounds behind the mountains
Green intimations unfurl the wind

    Koko   gba   kokodi
    Koko   didi   kokodi

III

IGI DA!
(THE TREE HAS FALLEN!)

Green, ever green, is the colour of our promise

IGÍ DÁ!

Atótó arére
Ìjàmbá baba fìtínà

Ẹ wá gbọ́ o,
Ẹ̀yin mùtúmùwà
Ẹ jẹ́ ká finúkonú
Ká ṣ'àpínrò ọ̀rọ̀
Ẹ jẹ́ ká sọ̀kò ọ̀rọ̀
S'áwọn aláàáké wọbìà
A-gé-tòní-má-ro-tọ̀la
A-sọ̀'gbẹ́-dasálẹ̀
A-sọ'lẹ̀-olómi-dìlú-òngbẹ

Ẹ jẹ́ ká w'òkè, ká w'ojú ọjọ́
Ká bi sánmọ̀n pé níbo l'òòrùn rè?

Igi ń tán lọ nínú igbó
Àgbọ̀nyín rọ̀bọ̀tọ̀ ti ń di àwátì lókè ọ̀dàn;
Erin ọ̀bátábatà a mi'gbó kìjikìji
Ẹfọ̀n a f'ìwo ràgàjà d'ẹrù b'ọdẹ tó gbóyà
Ẹdun a-bẹ́-má-balẹ̀, ànjọ̀nú orí igi

Níbo lẹ lọ?
Níbo lẹ̀yín wà?
Ẹ ba mi b'àwọn fọ́'gbó-fọ́'jù
A-gé-t'òní-má-ro-tọ̀la

Etí yín mélòó,
Ẹ̀yin aláàáké jẹgúdújẹrá?
Ẹrí ọkàn yín dà, ẹyin Agbégi-Mágbéyàwó?
Aginjù onígẹdú-góólù, onígi-òjé
Gbogbo wọn ti di pàrìfo asálẹ̀
Òrùlé ràgàjà t'éwé ta s'ágbègbè oòrùn
Ìyẹn ti d'ohun ìgbàgbé

À! gbágà! Igi ti dá
Ẹyẹ ti fò lọ
Ìrókò rògbòdọ̀, a fi gíga fìofìo ṣ'ẹ̀ṣọ́
Níbo ló wà?
Àràbà ríbí onígbòngbò rigiji ràgàjà
Níbo ló rè?

Ògánwó tó gan'wọ gan'sẹ̀ lọ́nà oko Abùsọrọ̀
Ta ló wó ẹ lulẹ̀ l'ọ̀sàn-án gangan gan-an?
Igi ọmọ̀ tó fún wa ní 'lẹ̀kùn ọlà
Níbo ló gbé dúró?

À! gbágà! Igi ti dá
Ẹyẹ ti fò lọ

Ẹ̀yin dà o,
Ẹ̀yin ọmọ Ọwá Ọba Igbó, Oba Ìgbẹ́
Ọ̀kẹ́rẹ́, a kéré, má kẹ̀rẹ̀, ọkọ ọyùnkún
Alágìrìwówó gbà wówó
Tó kọ́ 'le onífàráńdà sí 'nú gbò̀ngbò àràbà
Àkókóligi, ẹlẹ́nu gbẹ́gigbẹ́gi gbẹ́nàgbẹ́nà
Ògbìgbò tirigbò tirigbò

Ijọ́ eyín ká
N'ilé ẹ̀rín wó
Ijọ́ a f'igi ṣ'ọ̀fùn
N'ilé ìgbẹ́ d'ọ̀fo

À! gbágà! Igi ti dá
Ẹyẹ ti fò lọ

IGI DA (THE TREE HAS FALLEN)

Hear this, oh listeners, hear this:
Here comes Disaster, father of Trouble

Listen, oh listen
People of our land
Let us join minds
And reason our way ahead
Let us throw the stone of words
At the owners of the prodigal axe
Who cut and cut as if tomorrow does not exist
Who turn blooming forests into wastelands
And water-soaked terrains into famished regions

Let us look up
And ask: oh sky, where is the sun?

Tree stocks are vanishing in the forest
The big-chested barrigona[1] is disappearing without replacement.
So are the mountain-rumped elephant
The buffalo whose mighty horns affright the hunter
The monkey, magic acrobat on the tree top

Where have you gone?
Just where are you?
Let us ask the blind plunderers of the forest
Who cut and cut as if tomorrow will never come

Hear me well
You owner of the greedy axe
Where is your conscience, you wedded to wanton waste?
Once virgin forests with golden wood
Now ring out like hollow shells
The canopy which tames the raging heat
Has become a thing long forgotten

Alas, the tree has fallen
The birds have flown away

Majestic *Iroko*, lord of the heights
Where are you?
Araba which stands on top of spectacular roots
Where have you gone? *Oganwo*, loyal sentry on the road to Oke Abusoro

Who cut you down in the height of your noon?
Omo whose wood secures our door of wealth
Where have you stopped to balm your wounds?

Alas, the tree has fallen
The bird has flown away

Where are you now
You princes and princesses of the palace of the forest
Okere kere, husband of *Oyunkun*
Alagiriwowo wo wo wo
Who built a verandah-ed house between the flanks of *Araba*'s roots
Akokoligi who carves the wood with the dexterity of its restless beak
The red-head toucan can can too can[2]

The day the teeth depart the mouth
The house of laughter collapses
The day we kill the tree
We empty the forest of its irreplaceable wealth

Alas, the tree has fallen
The birds have flown away

AMAZON BURNING

(In the background throughout, drums, deep and dense
like the rainforest; flute with a faint tenor; both with varying
degrees of loudness. Mostly threnodic)

ACT ONE

Whose spark provoked this fire?

The Amazon is burning, burning , burning
Can you see the blaze
Sweeping like a raging storm
Across the roof of our Planet?

Dwellers of our Earth
Can you hear the deathly
Threnody of wailing leaves
In the inferno in the forest?

    The Amazon is burning
    The lungs of our Planet are seared by smokes

Do not ask me
Whose spark fathered this flame
Do not ask whose greed provoked the blaze
Do not ask whose blindness averted our gaze

From these incendiary graves.
We have sowed the tinder
These several seasons; here now
The horror of our long-awaited harvest

    The Amazon is burning
    The lungs of our Planet are seared by smokes

Tell it to our Emperors who fiddle
In their golden palaces while this earth
Burns and bleeds in countless places
Ever seen how they stumble on the clearest signs?

Sorcery trumps Science
A haughty superstition drowns the voice

Of genuine Reason: They who know nothing
Have become the masters of everything

The Amazon is burning
The lungs of our Planet are seared by smokes

We the Trees

We are the Trees of the Amazon
Ageless couriers of Earth and Sky
We traverse the darkest depths and loftiest heights
We, the branch and stem which sustain the world

Green, ever green, is the grace of our gift
Our coat of arms, our crown of wealth
We drape the earth in her vital robe
From looms so lush in their verdant lore

Behold the mothering massage
Of the lenient moss which hangs
From the greying branches like a sage's beard
And the ropy embrace by the vigilant vines

We cage the carbon from a careless Planet
That belches smokes like a congested chimney
The air we exhale in quick return
Is herb and tonic for a breathless world

We heal Earth's hunger and tame its thirst
The world stays secure in our steady shade
The rivers wiggle their way like majestic pythons
Through swaths beneath our blissful bower

We arrest the fury of the fatal wind
We brew the rain that sustains the fields
The laughter which comes at the season's end
Secures a place on the farmer's lips

Our carpet of mush and priceless dirt
Is magic manure for wandering growths

From the rustling chorus of fallen leaves
A tune beyond our mortal ears

Our leaves are open palms for the bene-
Dictions of the sun which ripens our fruits
From season to season till they drop
In obedience to the harvest call

From long, long, un-rememberable times
We have turned lean seasons into portly epochs
The victuals which sustain countless stocks
Are begging for the taking in our plenteous folds

Our leaves unload congested stomachs
Our barks will break your feverish bouts
Our roots will rout a thousand ills
In the countless ways we doctor the world

Those roots, our roots, traverse the tropics
Through deep down tunnels and alleyways
Way beyond the gaze of the hasty eye
We talk root to root in the parliament of the earth

We think, we dream, we dare, we talk at length
At times in whispers, other times in thunder
When the wind flutters our flanks into fanciful flutes
We sing and dance and defy the storm

We quarrel and kiss and flaunt our leaves
We lock our branches in sweet embrace
We do other things beneath the earth
Where roots touch roots beyond your gaze

Be gentle with your nerveless boots
As you plod through our crowded terrain
Be careful what you grab, for the vine may
Hide the difference between plant and python

Trees of the Amazon: here we are
Lungs of the Planet, crown on its head
We bleed when cut
Our wounds will wound the world

The I of the Tree

Kapok

My name is Kapok, Giant of the Amazon
They call me "Father of the Animals"
And they have never been far from right

Squirrels race up and down my body,
Their tails astir from my gentle breath
Monkeys come in their endless dozens,

Those restless gymnasts of forbidding heights.
The sloth, too lazy to climb, sometimes
Grunts its cheers from its humble patch

Three hundred years old, and still alive and green
My father saw many more moons, as also did my mother
My brood has long mastered the art

Of putting death beyond our gaze.
I tower above the earth in my journey towards the sky
Taming the sun's frightening fire with the magic of my leaves

Season after season, storms have come and gone
Some wild and furious with murder in every howl
But buttressed, hard as iron, I contain their murderous assault

Farmer, doctor, fortress, and spirit of the world,
I route the rain and direct the desert
I am that plug in the hole in the sky

   I am a vital lobe of the lung of the Planet

Ipe

A flurry of flowers, pink and proud
With pistils and pollens in the lofty air
This bright, bright acre in the rain's own region
Untouched by the dusken mood of a westering sun

This buoyant blossom in a season so unusually plain
Its tropical temper, its tenacious flare;

Not much room for spare leaves and hanging nests
But the parrot and the warbler still steal a spot

For their gossipy congress. The fruiteater goes home
Empty-handed from this pink campaign, its loss
The mouthful profit of the flycatcher
Probing every flank of the fragrant petals

Behold the deceptive tenderness of my wood
Whose iron timber defies the fire
And the ravaging edge of the conquering axe.
My flowery abundance that yields no ground to moth and mold

My bloom charms the seasons
Teases the sky, unwinds the wind
For the pinker my crowning glory
The greener its rich remembrance

   I am a vital lobe in the lungs of the Planet

Shiringa (Rubber Tree)

They named me Rubber Tree
For my rare, invaluable juice

My long, long blessing
Is a curse with countless cuts

Drip, drip drip
As I drain from moon to moon

From cup into can
From pail into vat

From serene forest fare
To friendless fiery factories

And the big-bellied billionaires
And their castles in the air

I guard their feet from thorns and thistles
Though I'm left with none to protect my own

I stretch the world from pole to pole
From rolling wheels to dizzying towers

I am the faithful roof they crave and court
For the rain and dust which besiege their days

My latex laughter is a lyric of tears
Its milk-white juice is red with rage

Ribbed with their rude desire, I bear
The scar of their latitude of lust

Ancient as the moon, resilient as the river
Neither Earth nor Sky can tell my age

They call me Rubber Tree for their venal interest
But the Forest calls me by my proper name

    I am a vital lobe in the lungs of the Planet

Cashapona (Walking Palm)

I surprise the forest floor with a welter of legs
Long, cane-like, and strong as steel

Leaning left and right, down and up
Reaching for my fair share of the tropical sun

Some think I rest by day and walk at night
Stepping gingerly on a load of leaves

The winkless tortoise and the snoring gecko
The double-natured bat and its clumsy somersault

Some think I stumble on the mouse
And challenge the cougar to a rapid race

Here I am swinging with the wind
Lavishly laundered by the evening rain

Stilt-dancer with a majestic sway
Envied by the millipede and its million limbs

I stand where I am
As I grow towards the sun

    I am a vital lobe in the lungs of the Planet

Barrigona

My name is Barrigona
(Some also call me Pona or Huacrapona)

My secret lives in the budge
I carry around my chest

Some think it is a pouch full of worms
Others swear it is bursting with gold

Only the Moon knows the secret
But the Ancient One will never talk

I bear a harvest of fruits
Hard-shelled, soft-cored

Delicious beyond compare:
The toucan's treat, the monkey's munch

I am never short of company
On my little patch of the forest

I adore the solid ground
For my roots are stiff and rugged

And so is my tempered stem
Unfazed by the army of worms and termites

In the palm's famous pedigree I have a place,
From Brazil to the Congo to Sulawesi

    I am a vital lobe in the lungs of the Planet

ACT FOUR

We bleed when cut

ALL

We are the Trees of the World
We are the Trees of Life
We laugh, we cry, we whisper, we shout
We breed, we brood, we breathe

We carry the Planet in our careful hands
A tender burden, historic task
The loom and latch of a naked world
We robe the Earth in our green embrace

Hour by hour we lose our kin
To waste, to war, and the senseless blaze
The careless axe, the haughty chain saw
And the cannibal greed of the rich and strong

Behold the Spider Monkey and the Spectacled Bear
The Butterflies, the Forest Crabs
The Eloquent Parrot, the Sagacious Owl
The Cool Canopy and the Travelling Roots

A Tree never falls alone in the forest
It takes our Future with the crashing leaves
The blind gold-digger, the reckless farmer
Subject your greed to the Need of All

We are the Trees of the World
We are the Trees of Life
Pearls from the Past, flowers of the Future
We burn when ignited, we bleed when cut

We are the vital lobe of the lungs of the Planet

Treetalk

Iroko greets the Oak

Obeche salutes the Elm

The Mahogany hails the Maple

Araba trades tall tales with the Red Wood

Green salutations, anxious whispers

"Why are so-called humans
So cruel with their axe",

The Olive
Asks the Cedar.

"Human", did you say?",
Retorts the Barrigona

Can't you see what they do
To their fellow humans?"

DEEP GREEN
(Once upon a Forest)

Deep green, my testament, as I forage
through this forest of vanished glories,
my memory one shell of naked echoes

Roots have shriveled in
earth's heat-harassed crypt
blighted leaves float in the wind
like flakes from careless scars

Long-limbed lumbermen have
laid low the loins of the land;
the Yes-I birds have left
with their rainbow songs

The desert marches towards the sea,
a haughty, implacable army . . .

Once (not too long ago)
I talked to trees in this forest
and trees talked back to me,

Deep green

IV

OUR DYING PLANET

Time long gone when
The earth was green and the seas were sane

ONCE UPON A PLANET

The sky above our head is
A ragged umbrella in need of a needle

The rain which leaks through the rupture
Is a cocktail of contending toxins

The cloud up there is a wet blanket
Dripping like a dirge upon a feverish earth

The birds fled several season ago
Without leaving a forwarding address

Prodigal saws have felled the joy
Of flourishing forests

There is a twilight stanza
In the song of the wind

Several seasons ago we sowed the Wind
The Whirlwind is ripe for our heedless reaping

The Earth we used to know
Is once-upon-a-time

CLIMATE OF FEAR

The rains come
too late these days
and leave before their time
withering fields foretell
the coming of furious famines

Spring swallows summer
summer stumbles into a sweltering fall
while winter joins the fray
with snowy deluge and blinding ice

Unstoppable fires consume the skies
from Kangaroo Island[1] to Paradise[2]

   Pause

A melting Arctic chokes the oceans
which claim the coasts and bury the cities
just one whittling whistle from the catacombs
of coral reefs bleached and buffeted
by a plague of acid and plastic debris

Once-in-a-century hurricanes
proliferate into ten-in-a-year
while countless typhoons pummel the peace
of once Pacific regions

Birds are falling from the sky
 lizards roasting on their rocky perch

Out of balance, out of breath
our Planet gasps and groans
as murky moons wobble their way
across the wilderness of a broken sky . . . .

   Pause

The earth we used to know
is once-upon-a-time.

MALINGERING MOUNTAIN?
(To the accompaniment of heavy drums and light flute)

The Mountain is slowly dying; they say it is just malingering. The Mountain which begat the hill; the hill which begat the hillock; the hillock which towers above the valley; the valley which mothers the flower; the flower which perfumes the wind; the wind which unwinds the trees.

Moon after moon after moon, they plundered the Mountain for its gold; harried the hill for its coal, foraged the flower for its scent, and the flower found the sun and the sun found the flower, and the sunflower's clockface spelt out the sun to its minutest tick, ramrod straight at noontide, long and slant with the westering shadows; furling, unfurling, furling unfurling; yellow loaves for the blue hunger of the sky; quiet with custom; penitent with the midnight moon.

The Mountain is dying
They say it's just malingering

And the rainbow's seditious stripes, its bended bout against the empire of the dark, its quickening quiver, its arrows sharp and sure in the archery of vigilant seasons. The Rain and the Sun, husband and wife, who kiss and quarrel, kiss and quarrel in their closet in the sky; from the thrill and thrall in the convenance of an arc, wondrous brow on the forehead of the sky, the laughing sky, the not-laughing sky, wondrous coalition of eyeful sounds, hue-ful harmony, music of the sweet supreme.

Rainbow, rainbow, Smile of the Spheres, luminous blend of water and wonder, Magic Arc of the endless Gaze

The mountain is dying
They say it's just malingering

And here comes the proto-call of the Parrot, flame-tailed, beak bent with boast and banter. Talkative talesman of the wild bush radio. Chitty chatter cha cha cha of the chant, the chant, the chant, the wind never weary, the leaves never tired of the swing and sway. Busy body, teasing tattler, scattering the forest's secrets like random seeds in the prodigal wind. Busy-beaked orator of the wild, unworried, where is your alphabet, where are your notes, where are the capricious characters of your mimic syllabary?

The Mountain is dying
They say it's just malingering

And the lake, the lake, too lean, too lonely now it never remembers its ancient lore; its squandered boast and bounce, its reach and range, its seamless schools of fishes surging, surging in its bold, voluminous waters, the flint-finned *alapandagi*, the block-headed *aro*, the fan-tailed *shawa*................, tutored by the rain, doctored by the wind, certified all sane until hostile skies unleashed the sun whose ferocious thirst undid the lake, till the pond was powder, the deed was dust, and a liquid paradise became an acre of bones and wails. Stench so strong it choked the sky.... And fishing boats flipped over into steamy coffins. The grass died and took its grace along. Bushels of dust where once were bowls of blessing. Swarming flies hover above the carnage. The wind coughed without remembering its throat.

The Mountain is dying
They say it's just malingering

Ask the night which fell like a pall over the moon; the moon which moaned like a mantra, songless many seasons, scorched by the searing sky, meandering through the clouds; the stars, now winking scars on the bicep of the night, wondering, just wondering where they left their laughter. A lingering darkness which surprised the bat, the bat with its viral virtuosity, its double-natured gymnastics, a COVID-captured world upsidedown, battered, breathless from a contagion so unhinged, so unhinging, veteran vampire so triumphant over its empire of death; and the owl, globe-eyed soothsayer of trembling temples, moping a fainting night into quickening dawn ....

The Mountain is dying
They say it's just malingering

The Arctic bleeds into the ocean the ocean swells and swallows the land the Sahara eyes the Amazon the Melaleuca trades yellow tears with the Kalimantan the Bijarim's green grace yearns for the sacred groves of Meghalaya the Congo coughs from an old, persistent plague the dark dense denizens of Ogbese telegraph urgent sighs to treetribes across the oceans fallen leaves bleed beneath our soles roots retching beneath the earth green crowns lost to senseless fires birds fleeing and flying fleeing and flying from the roostless inferno of our incendiary waste ....

The Mountain is dying
They say it's just malingering

The sky roasts before our gaze; the earth quakes beneath our soles; oceans choke from our toxic befoulments; from the fire and the fury, from so many seasons of incessant plundering, the Planet tells the tales of a time long gone when the earth was green the sea was silent fire was friendly the wind was wise the sky was sane.

The Mountain is dying
They say it's merely malingering

32

DYING LAKE

If things continue this way, what we now know as Lake Chad may disappear in fifty years* . . .

Who will listen
To the superstitions about the lake

To the deep-down darings
Of myths mightier than matter

Mysteries of half-told tales
Which swell the tongue

Of the rain; dark riddles
Of water faces with-

Out their masks.
A fiery drought burns

The helms of the lake's skirt
Her hidden treasure re-

Treating farther and farther
Into a frightened core

Too shrunk to read
The webbed calligraphy of ducks

Gliding blissfully on its thigh,
Broken reeds between their beaks

Frogtones fester into darktones
Beached shoals slap the nose

With a pungent guilt, mortally unaware
Of vultures hovering above the feast

More silt than salt
More sand than sense

A lake, once lush and lyrical
Lingers languidly

Between a song long forgotten
And a fever unseasonably fluid.

THE DESERT COMETH
(from a bird's eye view)

The desert
Marches towards the coast

Dust-faced
Fire-footed

A millennial fury in its gaze
A swath of scorpions in its hands

The sky: bare and frightening
The only cloud there is

Is a caravan of particles
And intimations of coming plagues

Wilted wheat
Unpunctual tubers

The Sahel unleashes its hell
The trees are in sad retreat

Between desert and ocean
A narrow strip of trembling green...

There is a fire hole
In the sky

Earth is nothing more than
A cauldron of dry dreams

KANINGO[1]

'This is what is left of my river'
—*Syl Cheney Coker*[2]

Is this what is left of that legend
that Cheney Coker sang about
the liquid lore that floated his magic lines?

Putrid now, gravely green,
constipated on a mongrel diet
of plastic castaways and rusting metals

The wide open bowl into which
the city empties its rumbling bowels
while the sky looks on in seamless consternation

How has a once amazing city
managed to survive the stench
of its rotting beauty?

Fish once frolicked in this river
while frogs heralded dawn's coming
with their raucous ululations

The birds which sang in the trees
traded notes with harps of verdant angels
leaves danced at the urging of the wind

Those were days when rain was no ruin
when children romped at the water's edge
and gentle breezes clipped the claw of tropical heat

Gone now, the legend and the lore
awaiting the rapid resurrection of
the river and the Land Entire.

VENICE UNDER WATER

Omi ya'le[1]
Agbara gba'gboro[2]

Rubber-boots, boatloads of anguish:
    The streets sulk and sigh
Beneath the roar
    Of a billowing floods

Saturated symphonies wail
    In the watery wind
The panting piano never knows
    What to say to the violated violin

The City of Shops and Shapes
    Sprawls haplessly on
In stark, amorphous misery
    Bloated books wade in search

Of missing pages.
    Famous antiquities shudder
In liquid silence, the museum a broken
    Reed in the riot of incorrigible rains

Blighted bistros, capsized tables
    Boated businesses, flotilla of franchise
Earth, that grossly abused Procurer,
    Here, at last, for its pound of flesh

Floating City, Adriatic Treasure,
    Tell me this when your lips are dry at last:
Who precipitated the climate of fear that has
    Turned these valuable streets into a rampaging sea?

MELODY UNHEARD

There is a melody to the wind
Heard only by the open ear

There is a tenderness to the flower
Felt only by the caring hand

There is a tallness to the tree
Seen only by those unafraid of leafy heights

There is a rhythm to the river
Measured in rustling whispers and liquid laughters

There is a music to the beauty of the earth
Treasured only by those with living ears.

THE SKY AIN'T BLUE

The sky ain't blue all the year, Baby
The sky ain't blue

Sometimes it is a messy boil above our heads
With a reddish aspect and pointless pain
Dire and dreadful and loath to burst

   The sky ain't blue all the year

Sometimes it is a wet blanket above our heads
With fraying edges and coarse, corrosive core
Heavy and broody like an ill-appointed pall

   The sky ain't blue all the year

Sometimes it is nothing more than a clump of clouds
Unmapped, unsure, a mere mossy plague
Dripping like a dirge for a half-remembered day

   The sky ain't blue all the year

Sometimes it is a canvas of prentice colours
A sploshy, splashy, squelching piece of painting
Final flourish to the rainbow's riotous parting

   The sky ain't blue all the year

Sometimes it is a tattered umbrella
With an epidemic of holes
Forever searching for an absent needle

   The sky ain't blue all the year, Baby
      The sky ain't blue

WE GLOW IN THE DARK

Oh so bright
We glow in the dark

The slick spokesman proclaimed
It's the safest source of power
Since the Almighty cracked the code of light

It burns no coal
It stokes no furnace
Cheap, clean power
Precious baby of triumphal Atom

·Its silos blend with the landscape·
Like proud pyramids in the land of the Pharaohs
You can build your house beside its fence
And wake every morning, safe and strong

Oh so bright
We glow in the dark

This smokeless fire lights the future's way
It powers the missiles the Empire needs
To keep the world in perpetual awe
The fail-proof elixir, the blaze and the bloom. . . .

Then something snapped
In the house of Science
The formulas went mad, and —
The core leaked its lethal juice. . . .

Nauseous winds, implacable plagues
The earth lays shriveled like rumpled foil
Behold how we roast like barbequed hogs
As we move from radiant to radioactive

Oh so bright
We glow in the dark
Glow, glow, glow
We glow in the dark

Now let thy servant depart in pieces
For their eyes have seen an apocalypse of ashes

HEAD IN THE SAND

(To the accompaniment of the song:
O ntan ra re je o
O ntan ra re je
Afasegbejo, o ntan ra re je[1])

Global warming is a figment
Of liberal imagination:

Melting Arctic ice
Is a dollop of cream in the sun

Rising oceans
Are bodies of water at play

That seven-year drought in Utah
Is just a dusty joke

The flood which buried the Koma village
Is a scene from Noah's epic

The desert's coastward march
Is a quest for a cool companion

   Afasegbejo o ntan ra re je

Seedless pods, treeless forests
Dewdrop dead and acid in the rain

Broiling winters, frigid summers
Toxic tub for global bath

   Afasegbejo on ntan ra re je

Belch out those carbons
Let factory fumes becloud the sky

That viscous streak on the delta creeks
Is beauty cream on the face of the sea

No price too high
For our glorious Progress

Stop crying wolf
You cowards of the Left

The future (if it comes)
Belongs to the strong and bravely blind

The science of your sense is way too weak
For the superstition of our creed

Global warming is nothing if not
A figment of liberal imagination

(The song in final flourish)

CORPSES THAT NEVER COUNT

We are people of the after-hours
Sundown shadows of the Empire that kindness forgot

Denizens of drought-denuded doldrums
We measure our days in bushels of dust

The forest, once gallant buffers
Between teeming towns and savage winds,

Now lie, neatly logged, waiting
For the one-way voyage to Liverpool

Seasons of suffocating aridity trade
Places with months of murderous deluge

Then came the floods
That washed our worth away

Poverty, Death's faithful envoy, enthralls
The land, obscene like a colonial sore

Used, then dumped like spent tickets,
Our corpses clutter the lanes

Like hordes of wingless termites
The day after a tropical rain

CANCER ALLEY

(To a quick, mock-martial tempo)

Welcome here to Cancer Alley
Where Death lives and thrives at a fixed address
With a fatal gallop, in a glittering dress
It combs the streets to boost its tally

Landfill Lane, ToxicDump Crescent
A boon from business, a mighty present
A puff of profit, the fantastic bribe
We're the Dead End dwellers, the chosen tribe

We drink our water, laced with lead
In our speck of dust a ton of dioxin
We live and die like yoked-up oxen
Oh how so blessed to be sorely bled!

There's a reddish vapour from my bedroom floor
From the frightened wall a yellow ooze
The Government Inspector discerns no flaw
Should the tenants move there's a lot to lose

Highway 10 is above my roof
The railtrack splits my blessed garden
For my deafened ears I need no proof
The music of my life is eternal din

A chemical plant blooms by my fence
My breath is a fare of fumes and smokes
A battered warrior without defence
My heart is a rubble of stress and strokes

Here's the Coughing Cradle, the Asthma County
The cracked-up kidney, the wasted liver
Lungs perforated like a riddled reefer
In the Dead End Zone, what a blissful bounty!

Pause

Three-fingered hands two-headed babies one-legged frog birds with missing wings fatal floods vengeful droughts hole in the sky hole in the sky hole in the sky in the sky in the sky hole in the sky the river caught fire hole in the sky the river caught fire hole in the sky in the sky in the sky hole in the ...

Pause

Welcome here to Cancer Street
The City's Waste Dump, and its pitch-Black death
They punch our sky, hazard our health
The earth is fire beneath our feet

REFUGEE CAMP

The obscene painscape of the refugee camp
Its tattered tents, its pestilential scourge

Air heavy with rancid breaths
Garments garnished with authentic lice

Weeping wounds
Broken dreams

Diarrhea dialogues and malaria motions
Death comes at ten for one penny

Birthcries pierce the silence of morbid nights
Beside dumpsites where germs breed in reckless millions

Ears tuned to the music of breaking waters
Emergency midwives ease the labour of panting moments

Red Cross trades mercy missions with Red Crescent
Their ears primed to the beat of desperate hearts

Shifting shapes, dislocated affinities
From the marble mansion of yesterlife

To the common dust of prefabricated slumhood.
Disaster, Destiny's daughter, staggers into the fray,

Wild, veiled, and many-tongued,
Spawning doubts and mortal fears.

A widowed woman gazes at the shifting sky:
"Are you still there, God of Infinite Mercy"?

ACT OF GOD

Nothing act-of-god in this
Nothing

Nuclear plants on the brow
Of quaking mountains

Coal ash in the river
Which minds the village need

Mountains scooped and savaged
By improvident greed

Forests lumbered into extinction
And the consequent lumbago of an ailing earth

The coastward march of the desert
And rising oceans which consume the land

Stubborn cancers
Which belie the healer's genius

Carbon plague in the air
Hole in the sky

Here goes the tale of the bird
Which pollutes its nest

Cho cho cho the bird
Which pollutes its nest

Nothing act-of-God in this
Nothing

ECO-SNAPS

A tale of Two Prayers
or
Two Ways of Looking at the Sky

The sky is hot as a furnace
The lawn's grass droops into sickening brown

Cornfields are withering
Rivers shrink into serpentine streaks

A season this dry and dangerous
They have never seen on this Edenic island

But while the natives pray for rain
The tourist longs for everlasting sunshine

Fog-fraught

Fog fog fog
Fog everywhere

I cannot see my navel
I cannot see my neighbor

I cannot see the day
I cannot see the sky

The city is choked and retching
The people are scared of breathing

I cannot see the Government
I cannot see tomorrow

V

REDEMPTION ARMY

Green shields, rainbow warriors

REMEMBERING KEN SARO WIWA

(To a brisk, somewhat martial beat)

I saw brave Ken the other night
Short and sharp like an angry song
So many years, still no respite
The rot so rife, the pain so strong

The Oil Tycoons still pollute the land
Like a bunch of braggarts, untouchable band
Our days still dark, our nights a-flare
Our lives are ruled by fright and fear

The creeks are clogged, the rivers are choked
The fish are dead, the crops are gone
The same old fires, so blindly stoked
The same Oil Men with the greedy gun

They drill and drill and still they drill
A prostrate earth their mighty thrill
They spare no thought for coming years
Our trampled land, its wears and tears

The Delta's Black Gold, our yellow threat
Our plundered land and corrupted home
They scoop their billions without a sweat
The polluted people are the rusted chrome

The story, dear Ken, is still the same
Except in places it's grossly worse
The Delta's door shakes in its feeble frame
The rot's too strong for my humble verse

FOR GRETA THUNBERG

T'agba ba nse bi omode
Omode a maa se bi agba[1]

   "How dare you?!",
   She asked.

The riveting thunder of her question
Rattled the roof of a sleepy world.

In her belly a compelling volcano
Urgent with fearless fire

In her mouth
The tongue of Sage and Seer:

Listen to the tree
Respect the river
Tame that Greed which consumes OUR world
Give OUR Earth a chance to live

   "How dare you?!",
   She asked.

From pole to pole, that thunder
Nettled powerful naysayers

Who lost every sense
Of the Reason behind her Rage,

Its impatient indignation
Its roaring, redemptive reproach.

   "How dare you?!",
   She asked.

The Women of Greenham Common[2]
Nodded in grateful remembrance. . .

Our Universe rocks
   To the rhythm of her courage

The Future
    Sways to the vastness of her vision

"How dare you?!",
    She asked.

THE DELTA SINGS BETWEEN THE TIDES

The river no longer
Sleeps in its bed

Its pillow is now
A cradle of broken skulls

Legendary JP
Cannot count the casualties

In the frightened waters,
Though season after season

He has watched the moon toss and turn
Like the proverbial reed in the tide

The Nun, ravaged by ruthless rigs,
Now crawls tiredly towards the sea

Even as her remnant virtue
Lingers languidly in Okara's majestic verse

When last did you hear the moans
Of Omoja whose beneficence nourished

Ojaide's songs when his years were young
And the rains were rich and real?

Crying creeks, violated valleys
Toxic cocktail of cannibal cartels

Quenchless, like Ifowodo's Oil Lamp
Blinding, like Ikiriko's Oily Tears

We all thought it was oil
But Bassey saw the blood behind the boom . . . .

Dark days
Nights fraught with flares

Omens without Amens
Strange like a seven-headed plague

FOR IBIWARI IKIRIKO

(And River Nun)

Okara paddled his verse
through your silver-faced majesty
probed the poetry of your silence
and sang songs which echoed

In the Delta of your dreams.
That was long ago
when your waters were clean/free
when your nights were dark

And your days were bright
Now you lumber like a drunken
python towards the sea
your fishes frightened

Your aspect unclear
Oil-choked and viscous with vices
Your song this time is
sad like a rotten crab

Caucuses come and go
in the government house
fat on talk, lean on truth
even as you lie so broken,

   So unchaste...

But the poet shouts the names
Of the authors of your anguish

INVOCATION
(Mardi Gras 2010)

Call: E maa pe ko se (All say let it be)
Response: Ase (Let it be)

Oh Sky
Throw open your door

Let the Sun dance across
The threshold of the opening day

The morning dew honors the grass
With its crystal halo

Virgin paths crave the touch
Of rising feet. Magic mists on mountaintops. . .

Those who passed have never parted
Those who passed have never parted

Their voices rouse the echo in the hills
Their river throbs in our living veins

Those passed have never parted

In the beginning of the beginning of the beginning
In the unbroken/unbreakable ring of being

In the fire that burns and never dies
In the rag which outlasts the wardrobe

In Memory, mother of Remembrance
Let this day anchor our scattered songs

Spirit of the Wind, Spirit of Singing Waters
Spirit of Earth-Mother, Spirit of Sky-Father

Spirit of Talking Drums and Dancing Trees
Spirit of Feet that never forget their soles

Spirit of the Word, Spirit of Silence
Spirit of Ancestors in rainbow garments

Let the Eagle perch, let the Kite perch
Let the world have the peace of the stream at dawn

Guardians of the Flame
Secure the Blaze

Secure the Blaze
Secure the Blaze

Guardians of the Flame
Secure the Blaze

Let it light a path
Across the universe

Those who passed have never parted

E maa pe ko se
Ase

MANY STARS, ONE SKY

Oruku tindi tindi
Oruku tindi tindi[1]

Many stars
   One sky

A pageant of colours
      One rainbow

Many trees
   One forest

A medley of songs
   One choir

Oruku tindi tindi

Many fingers
   One hand

An array of tongues
   One language

Many threads
   One robe

A throng of peoples
   One world

Oruku tindi tindi
Oruke tindi tindi tindi tindi tindi. . . .

ECO HINTS

When last did you
    Hear a river cry
From the lethal pain
    Of arsenic poisoning

What did you do
    When your favourite lake
Turned from blue to purple
    Then to frightening red

When last did you
    Sigh at the swansong
Of a falling tree
    And the empty agony of shadeless terrains

The rain, these days,
    Is fire from the sky
The roof knows its rage
    The earth its flood

A tree falls in Congo's forest
    An iceberg crashes
In the distant Antarctic
    Dreadful chain of our dying Planet

The oceans choke on plastic
    A mercury plague un-schools the shoals
There is a blazing hole in the sky
    Unseen by the Blind-in-Power

VI

BOUNTY

From green grass to brown bread

FOR WORLD FOOD DAY

This ode to:

The clan of yams,
Swollen feet of gallant vines

Fresh-dug potatoes
Glistening in the sun

The race of rice
Golden crown of giggling grass

The brotherhood of wheat
Rising, rising in the furnace of the sun

The sorority of cow peas
With delicious antimony in each eye

The tribe of tomatoes
Succulent paradise, sinfully red

Rain-roused spinach
In league with lettuce

The pawpaw's pendulous promise
Hearty laughter of sinless apples

And the Sea so generous
With its boundless treasures

And forests brimming
With inestimable bounty

Oh, the sinuous symphony of winnowing winds. . . .

With green fingers and brown baskets
We keep Hunger in permanent exile

(2014)

OBA L'AGBE[1]

All hail the farmer
Who puts hunger to flight,
Sows laughter on our lips,
And tends the fields from moon to moon

Fruiting trees tilt earthwards,
With their joyful burdens
Fattening tubers are singing
In the belly of swollen heaps

The plantain plants a smile
In the compost of passing seasons
Cow peas drape the furrows
With leguminous flourish

The tomato tribe rolls on the ridges,
Soft in their whisper, jolly in their juice;
Pumpkins rump in the sun,
All-round pleasure, a succulent delight

Corn-cobs throb in
The loins of expectant stalks
Their silky tassels swaying
In the ripening sun

And then, the market's prodigious fare
Dappled stalls, brimming bowls,
Bargaining banters, irrepressible music
Flotilla of flavours, a caravan of colours

Behold the back-breaking hoe
The hand-corroding machete
Sun-stroke and rain-drench
The plough and the pain

All hail the Farmer
Master of the Dew[2], Friend of the Rain
Hands which stir the soil
Spirit of eternal harvests.

SONG OF LIFE (2)

E wa woo o (Oh come and behold)
Ereke l'aye wa (The path to pleasure is in the mouth)

Call me when the full pot
Is singing in the fireplace
Its bottom licked red
By the tongue of the flame

Call me when the delicate
Trinity of tomato, thyme, and turmeric
Raises a sacred song
In the pious corner of the hungry kitchen

Rodo, sombo, ata wewe, ata ijosi[1]
Crazy crayfish and the crazier crab
The bulbous onion which teases us
To tears with layers and layers of delight

Merry marriage of venison and mutton
Shuggling shanks, succulent breast
Bounteous *bokoto* and the Sir which loins
The brood of dancing chunks

Call me, kind soul, call me
If we cannot meet above the thigh
We shall meet somewhere around the ribs
If not the wings, then surely, below the neck

Call me over, call me in
Lead me by the nose, unwind my tongue
Let me sing a song
For the Deity of the Guts

ODE TO THE PINE APPLE

Praise the Pine Apple
Mother of joyful juice
Queen who sits so pretty on a paradise of gold
Tasty treat, wonder to be-hold

On your head a crown
Of spiky fronds and famous flowers
In your belly the water of life.
The origin of that water

Only the Rain has the mouth to tell:
The Rain, Daughter of the Cloud
The Cloud, scion of the Sky
The Sky, sister of the Sea

The Sea, spirit of the Seasons. . .
Your body all spikes
Your flesh smooth like the moon
Your blood sweet and tempting like

The wine of the gods
Close to the earth,
Low as a shadow
The white man's palm[1]

Though you bear no kernels
For the squirrel's relentless teeth
And the wine in your belly
Provokes no foam or fury

Oh Apple Pine,

You sit on a table
And the table shakes with delicious splendor
The kitchen sprouts an armory of knives,
All so intoxicated by your sweet, forbidding legend

Drop drop drop
Drop that juice
In the paradise of my mouth
There is a tropical temper

In the flavour of your laughter
Once stubbornly green
Now a yellow yes
The sun which provoked the journey

Is still in its fiery sky
I touch you with my eye
I see you with my nose
Oh Pine Apple, generous as a genie

You who built a house of honey
Whose walls are made of thorns

THE WATER MELON OF HARGEISA
(for Jama)

You tease my morning pleasure
With the red laughter of
The water melon of Hargeisa

The green skin of a balm
Which lurks in the core
Where the juice's just dessert

Salves the wizened throats
Of peripatetic patriarchs who carry
The Word between their sighs

Melon of the gods
Liquid mercy of desert priests
Who climb to the sky

On a ladder made of prayers.
My thirsty soul blesses the spirits who quench
Raging fires with the water of friendship

Hargyesa melon, oh so heavy
With the water of kindness,
Red like Freedom's Road

STRING BEAN
(for Dave Brinks)

I thread through the knots of my string bean,
praying for the instant banishment
of the pandemic of hunger

A shower of corngrains
unsettles the taciturn roof
above my temple of abstinence

Even though it's the Season of the Fast
and the sun must not see
us open and close our mouths

We still need to shame
future pains and pangs
with the bounty of our bravery

MY KITCHEN IS A GARDEN

My kitchen is a garden
   With brimming baskets
Of contending fruits
   Waiting for the willing hand

In this crowded galaxy
   Are star apples of Eden
Pompous pears pampered
   By the upland sun

The heart-shaped avocado
   Once secret consort
Of passionate leaves, green
   Like a soft unspeakable sin

There is also kiwi
   Of the *kiwon-kiwon*[1] clan
Whose rough-raw exterior
   Is sheer prolegomenon to its hidden delight

And the pendulous pawpaw
   Swinging, swinging, swinging
Amid the trumpet leaves
   In the merciful melody of early rains

It is the carrot's calling
   To rouse them all to riot
While the cucumber, cool as ever,
   Is well known for its versatile deployments

HARVEST

Rose petals in the wind
The arrow is quivering in its quiver

I will send you
seven rains and seven winds
plant behind your house

A garden
of butterfly angels and
flowers with petals of paradise

Bees which endow their hives
and fragrances which lead
the seasons by the nose

I will build you,
a room in the vent-
ricle of my heart

Untouched
by the wasting war
of wind and water

The sun will never hesitate
in its journey across our brows.
We who sow the earth

Will reap the sky

VII

SEASONS

Green, yellow, and other mooncantations

WARNING

The dry season is here again
Leaves fall like golden tears
From the eye of the forest

Rivers have suspended their song,
The choir of frogs vanishing behind
The dry wall of the moon

The harmattan powders curious faces
With the grey memory of distant regions
Roads revel in dusty excess

The dry season is here again;
Wayfarers beware:
Mating antelopes ahead...

HARMATTAN

Its mirth is mist
Its touch is grey

It carries dry ice
On its fingertips

It lives in a room
In the house of the wind

Early-year caller
With cracks on lips

A pot of cream
For our famished skin

Our days are hot
Our nights are cold

Needles in the wind
Clouds in the sky

It's the Northeastern caller
With dust on every toe

The farmer's friend
Ripener of the pea

Bringer of the chill
That tames the heat.

FALL FELLOWS

When the autumn wind has (finally)
silenced the cicadas
and the shrieking choir
drops wing after wing
to the chilly laps
of an all-embracing earth

The assiduous squirrel
will stop, tail mid-fluff,
foreclaws holding up an acorn
like the hands of a praying priest
at the season's recurrent communion

Lake ducks know not
what to make of the hasty hostility
of a once friendly water,
now chilly like an ill-remembered joke,
the brood clucking behind the matriarch
like refugees from a vanquished epoch

YELLOW YAWN

Autumn yellowed dawn's river
with the philosophy
of a nervous yawn

Rainbowed a colourless noon
with a polyphony of
songs and sundry musings

The evening snored
into night in
the hammock of my dream

Sleep came down
in isolated syllables
on the lips of trembling pillows

Breaking waters
push a poem in the mater
nity of laboring rocks

TIMID SEASON

Here, too, the stones wept
when the river took off its clothes

and the mountains shifted their gaze
with prudish disdain

Shoes still quarrel with friendly feet
on roads which laugh through their dusty teeth

The season thrives
under its carapace of silence

On an evening which eavesdrops
the whispers of a nervous night

The frangipani is singing again
my dusken nose hears its melodious fragrance

Far, far, there in a liquid sky
a timid season is still learning

How to kill two stones with one bird

AUTUMN IN NEW HAMPSHIRE

I

The sun strikes a match
In the yellow corner of the sky

Forest tops are aflame
With autumnal splendour

The maple laughs its joy
In orange and running red

A shy green lines the upper lip
Of the tumbling valley

Like the thin moustache
Of a sprawling giant

And the leaves, dancing in the wind

Squirrels count their blessings
In the balding heights, their nutty tales

Fluffy episodes in the narrative
Of the wind; the mallard duck

Glides on the chilly lake (how I
Envy its webbed mastery of water!)

Moose moss is falling; deer district
Is yellowing into a yell. Though the pines

Still sing green at noon, their needles
Sticking young to their ageless heads

And the leaves, dancing in the wind

As it did last season
And the season before

The Monadnock watches it all
From an earthy distance

Its spine still tattooed
By the footprints of summer pilgrims

The letters of its legend
Never fall with changing moons

Its dialogue with the New England sky
Is as old as the ravens on its ribs

And the leaves, dancing in the wind

II

Pumpkins rolling in the furrows
Their vines dry like shrunken vows

The melon so mellow it forgets the knife's
Smooth dance through its crumpled skin

The nectarine still keeps wondering
What debt it owes the bee

The plum plunges, unscathed,
Into the cave of waiting baskets

And the leaves, dancing in the wind

The apple's song survives the ages
From the unbitten chant of hip hop divas

To the unheard melody of Eve
Who taught the world the way to eat

Red, red runs the rhythm
Of the fall, the liquid fire

Of drifting leaves,
The copper choir of harvested fields

And the leaves, dancing in the wind

EARLY SPRING IN CITY PARK

Northern winds have beaten a cold retreat
to their Arctic roost

The oaks, ever so (a)live,
break into olive sweat,

Their moss, Spanish and smoothly grey,
swinging soberly like a griot's beard

New poems erupt
at the end of silent branches

Their music mellow
from the green prosody of the wind

A joyous squirrel ruffles the air
with its restless tale

Its pranks lean, its chuckling
one moon from mature laughter

My eyes memorise these lines
from the book of a wild awakening

The hibiscus's precocious budding
a riot of pollens seeking anchor in friendly places

The throaty serenade of mallard ducks
gliding enviably on the chilly lake...

   (Summer's song is still a foliage away)

I encounter the sun's resurrection
in the leafing Galilee of Louisiana oaks

SPIRIT OF SPRING
(for Mary Jay)

...snowdrops, crocuses, and daffodils came again, and the air is now beautiful...
Spring makes one feel all over again that life is for living too![1]

Break out with the Spirit of Spring
Crack earth's crust with the tip of your song
Hone every tune to the frolic of the frost

Perfume your fancy with the voluptuous elegance of the tulip
Range rich and raw like its unfolding glory
Brighten your laughter with the lilt of the lily

All budding beauty, earth;
A festival of blossoms, petals twirling grass-
Wards on the innocence of the wind

Your olive touch awakes the lawn,
Its crystal memory stirring valleys and leafing heights
Quickening ashes into flares, murmurs into melodies

   Break out with the Spirit of Spring
   Rouse Earth to song with your magic string

QUEST-IONS (3)

Behold the lily in your garden
How white are its teeth
In the mirror of the August rains

Behold the pumpkin
Creeping in the green lane
How fast is its limbless race

Ask the chameleon which harvests
Its hues from a fair of different forests:
Who cut your coat of many colours

Behold the smokes
Snaking skywards above the chimney
How happy is the fire they left behind

Behold the dream which leapt
From the bed and hit the road
How many night's mares obstruct their gallop

Ask the moon
Which drips into the rippling ocean
How many drops will sail a ship

Behold the curse
Which winds round the tongue
How many serpents can it slay

Behold the tear painfully planted
In the compost of our joy
When will it sprout a lyric full of laughter?

NIGHT WINGS

The night does not know
What to do with the mottled squadron

of mosquitoes droning
like programmed jets
on murderous missions

and fireflies daring
the dense impenetrability of night
with their yellow peril.

Blind with inordinate daring,
moths swarm the lamp-post
with a brittle passion

even as bats, shriek-throated acrobats,
stab night's ears with their
furtive, ambivalent moaning

The wind is witness to it all
the sky a slow runway with
a floodlight of sighing stars

Little things fly big
and the sky knows not what
to do with its squadron of wings

POLYGAMOUS MOON

A polygamous moon cannot manage
her plague of husbands
nodding claims stand stiff

In lunar closets, or hang limp
on the tree of a penitent wardrobe
jealous rays unravel

the chastity of the night
Desire bathes her wrinkles
In the pitcher of a pagan milk

Night so dark, so hot
even nouns forget their names
a retinue of adjectives plays

Clown in the courtyard of liquid shadows
flowing back, flowing forth
like the robes of eating chiefs

The moon, polygamous still,
her roster crowded with passionate longing
her sweat scented with nameless things

Knowing not what to do with the night's
inky consort, and a bevy of stars
winking coquettishly at the waiting stallions

THE MOON WHO CAME TO MY GARDEN

The moon came to my garden at night;
it being the season of the Northeast Trades,
the earth was dry the sky all drained
the Harmattan shared its dust
among the winds

The moon came to my garden at night,
scaling my flower fence and wall of mists
a gentle rustle, a wary rasp,
then a tell-tale giggle of fallen leaves
(the twigs were too tangled to talk)

I slid open the door of my eyes
peeped through sleep's blue window
and dispatched a yawn-yoked shout
across a fragrant silence;
petals creaked like October crickets

My voice caught the moon
on a big ripe orange;
she shot through the leaves
and vanished through the clouds,
leaving beside the pumpkin pile:

    a bouquet of smiles
        &
    a millennium of milk

VIII

WIND WATER AND
PUNCTUAL PETALS

So proudly green in all your aspects

WIND

There is a heavy timbre
To the tenor of the wind

Trembling leaves hold
Their heads with both hands

Trees butt baffled gusts
Like rams too drunk

On the divinity of their horns
Never seen roofs rock

So languidly without rolling;
The drum this day is dread

There is a metallic roar
In the sermon of the storm

The son in the song
Is the father silence.

THE RAINMAKER'S DAUGHTER

I am
the Rainmaker's daughter
my fingers are made of water

Conceived in the clouds
when the sky was half asleep
birthed by the wind

In the silence of a storm
my legs are shafts of showers
my eyes dewdrops on friendly grass

I sent the valley
on an errand; the valley came back
with a nest of singing rivers

Whose bank is green
with rumours of my soft affairs;
trees, wary as warriors,

Protect the water's edge.
The streamside grass
is my lush eye brow

I am
the Rainmaker's daughter
I dance on every roof

The rhyme and rust of tingling
zinc, the corrugated laughter
of dripping heights

I am
the Rainmaker's daughter
spirit of the ripening corn,

The kicking tuber,
the murmuring melon,
crystal raindrops on banana leaves

I am
the Rainmaker's daughter
foe of fire, friend of the flame

DEWDROP (1)

The dew has wings
but it cannot fly
beyond the grass

There are grey tears
on the morning's face still
heavy from the burden of sleep

Inchoate whispers perch
on the sky's ears
tremulous like nervous vows

In the vanished garden
behind the Mountain of the Moon
wilting buds pray for quickening drops

The sky gathers its robe
its helms dripping
with breaking water

DEWDROPS (2)

Dewdrops
Drop drop dew drops

In our childhood days
We thought they were
Tearful joys of Heaven
Shed by the sky before
Sleeping Earth could open its eyes

Dewdrops

Rain which came without a hint
Quiet as a covenant; cool as courage
The grass's crystal crown
Liquid silver of a tender lore
Dawn-brewed, beaded with bubbles

Dewdrops

Showerless blessing, the farmer's friend
The field's first sip
Before the rain's raw deluge
Its quiet kindness,
Its quickening touch

Dewdrops

In my childhood days
Dawn was kind and cool
Before a mercury menace undid the dew
Now the sky's eyes are red
Dawn's whisper is louder than its shout

Dewdrops
Drop drop dew dew drops

WATER

Water has its own language
:

When it talks
The rain listens
The cloud claps

The river reels
And rolls with laughter
The lake never knows

What to do with its excess of grace
The streamside is a choir
Of waving ferns

Water has its own language
:

When swollen into flood
Its fury is brown
(And crimson-deep in parts)

It races through the streets
On legs forever unseen
Grabs everything in sight

With hands beyond the eye
It befriends the sky,
Purloins its thunder

Water has its own language
:

And teeth filed with salt
And ears waxed with words
And tongue forked with tales

Its tale is
Long as the Nile
Massive as the Mississippi

Parting continents
Coupling countries
Native of a thousand I-lands

Water has its own language
:

In the dark seal-ables
Of the season
Of the sun

Of the wind's sweeping war-
Rant, the rolling boulder
From the upland quarry

And the slow, slow
Dance in the region
Below the mountain

Water has its own language
:

Its Robin-Hood morality
Its shifting fortunes
Its partial largesse

Between waste and want
Plenty and penury
And the thirsty threat

Of looming sands
Fish learn, often too late,
The mortal ambiguity of water

RIVER

How does one count
the legs of a running river
:

mountain-sprung
frothy-free

racing through
cliff and crag

smoothing rough
heady boulders

into swift
relentless eggs

gently slowing towards
the old, alluvial plains

magic melody of heels
so faithful, so unseen

of serenading sands
and banks with liquid songs

THE LAKE WHICH FORGOT ITS CLOTHES

The lake left home without its clothes
Courting prying eyes with the succulence of its sighs.

Its poignantly proportioned aspects
Caught the mid-day sun at its brightest moment.

Its stride and surge
Was joy-talk for the busy birds

Geeky ducks plied its surface
With the world-wide web of their feet

Provoking ripples which map out the globe
In whirls of liquid wonder

Ah, the day the lake left home without its clothes
The sky laughed through its wardrobe of clouds

A PADDLE MADE OF WORDS

after reading Stanley Moss's "Anonymous Poet"[1]

I'd never sailed so eloquently
until the day your tongue
became a lake

(Y)our banter built a boat with a forest of nouns
we beat several consonants

into a paddle as we watched vowels fall vow after vow, dissolving noise-
lessly in the waiting water

Between us a silence untouched by the baying moon
and her syllables of sin

Together we seek a baptistery for the innocence of a nameless dream.

LILY

How does one count
The teeth of a laughing lily

:

Burrow through
The passion of its petals

Pluck every bullet
In the barrel of its pistil

Flick its filament
Which turns on the sun

Like a blooming bulb
Dance through the brown

Dentistry of its drought
Slice the air

With the green sword
Of its leaves. . .

Rinsed by the rain
Its laughter glistens like a vow

Haughticulturally
Alive

MAGNOLIA (1)

So proudly green, your leaves,
in this hot, heady season

So raw the raspy symphony
of the winds which

pranced over the Prairies,
galloped down the mountains

Stole their way down to the Gulf
with chilly tributes from the Tundra King

Your glossy glory, your copious shade
even while the maple drifts skywards,

Its branches bare, forlornly silent.
Here, still, a roost for the squirrel

For the soft-beaked pelican, for the trumpet-
coated cicada waiting for its autumn concerto

When, like white loaves, your flowers
are feast for the eye, song for the sun

Magnolia so magnificent
Your jazzy juice, your raspy riffs

Your song so South,
how so light you look now

With no strange fruit
or dangling burdens

MAGNOLIA (2)

Generous loaves
sizzling between the leaves

Baked by the sun
Laundered by the rain

Layer after layer
Of punctual petals

Egret-white
Sumptuous as a sigh

One idle day
In the hungry glare of a summer noon

In awe-ful silence
And fervent curiosity

Let desire sate its sigh now
Before this wonder wrinkles into ruin

Before the sky bows to the yellowing
Call of an unforgiving fall

GBARIJO[1]

Shall we also talk
about the rain
which gathers us all
beneath the roof of its mercy

Or the sympathetic laughter
of thunder which teases
the etiquette of our ears?

All things scatter
that are capable of gathering
behold the rude reality

Of the noonday sun
which disperses the conspiracy
of soldier ants

But how can the forest
convoke the trees with every head
wrapped in a separate halo

Sometimes
life behaves like
a market in its closing hours.

IX

GREEN RESOLVE

All things green – and beautiful

WISHES

(Drumtaps plus flute and/or sax)

Wish I could *still* laugh with the lotus
On the bank of the Nile

Take off my clothes
And dive into the Zambezi

Join spirit dancers
In the middle of the Ganges

Romp with the Rio
To the thunder of the samba

Fan the Yangtze's face
With the feathers of the moon

Tease the Thames
With a shoeless foot

Embrace the Volga
With open arms

Ask the Mississippi
For a bowl of water . . . .

Alas, between cup and lip
An acre of wishes

CONNECTED

If you fell a tree in the Amazon forest
Its sigh may light a fire in the Arctic ice

If you pour coal ash into the Mississippi
It may maul the minnows in the Limpopo

If you stir the mud of the Titicaca
You may provoke eerie ripples in the Ontario

If you start a bushfire in Fiji
The smokes may unease the sky in Sidney

If you provoke a sneeze in Kensington
It may spark a cold in Kisangani

Chernobyl's fatal fumes share a dangerous ancestry
With the lethal leaks of Three Mile Island

Seeds we all are in a common pod
Sharing one earth, beneath a common sky,

Act of God
Is act of wo/man

REMEMBER
(Flute: soft & mellow)

Does anyone still remember

That little earthworm wiggling its way
Across the path at dawn

The snail inching up the tree
Its shell a knapsack of colourful whorls

The flair in the fin
Of anonymous shoals. . . .

The whale's virulent migraine
In the infirmary of troubled waters

Does anyone remember

The terror in the tiger's tale
Which curtails the grace of the leaping deer

Ants' serpentine columns
At the root of the grass

The funereal rasp
Of the leaves of falling forests

The mountain's *rigor mortis*
The last sigh of sleeping seas

The quiet footsounds
Of Earth's Redemption Army

Can anyone re-member?

DARE-DO

I tie a rope
   to the edge
     of the sun

And fly it
   like a kite
     across the sky

I beam my eyes
   on a fiesta
     of flowers

When I fling open the window
   my room is
     full of light

The moon
   is a candle
     on my bedside table

The grass goes
   green
     wherever my rain has touched

STUBBORN HOPE

(after Dennis Brutus;
and in honour of those wonderful human beings
in the Mercy and Care Community)

There is something about it all
That tugs at the heart of our (un)common humanity

The unfathomable vulnerability of the earth
Which rumbles beneath our feet

The cacophony of catastrophe
Which unsettles the music of the mind

Crimson wails congealing
In the ears of wounded moments

Running sores of stories
Told and retold by toothless mouths. . . .

Shadows hide the day
The devil's dark laughter

Unnerves the ears
Of the noonward sun

    Pain walks in the streets

But

A stubborn hope sustains our being
A kindness which seeks neither gold nor garland

Intimations of another sky beyond
Tattered tents and their ribs of bones

A stubborn hope which unlocks the door
Of the house that Laughter built

The future needs a tongue of iron
To tell the tale of these uncanny catastrophes

EMBERS

Beneath these ashes
   A choir of sighing embers

Hope
   thin-bodied

Is bent
   not broken

HOMECOMING

The elephant grass was witness
To our first homecoming
In that splendid savannah of our youth

It all happened in the period of the waning moon
Cornfields were laughing with the early rains
As yellowing mangoes swung green between the leaves

The silkcotton tree over-saw our care-less laughter
In the latitude of a decisive season
When flowers perfumed the evening sky

We have run with the river
Laughed with the lake, overheard the dew-
Laden whisper of the roadside grass

The mountain is our bread
The well-watered valley our basket of bliss
The forest's green glory our rainbow garland

From the road we learnt
The divinity of distance, far,
Yet not so far, the fallacy of absence

Moon after moon after moon
We ripen beneath the tempering sun
Our song is rain which forgives the drought

STILL WE SING
(With solemn, deliberate music)

Still we sing
   of life beyond the geography of pain
      far from the quaky temper of violated mountains

Still we sing
   of rivers proud of their water
      of forests which adore their trees

Still we sing
   of the melody of the light which embraces the dawn
      the breeze which pulls the beard of ageing palms

Still we sing
   of the rain which provokes the seeds
      the conspiratorial canopy of laughing leaves

Still we sing
   of the invincibility of the human spirit
      the laughter which survives the storm

Still we sing
   of a Planet sane and sound
      of all things green - and beautiful.

NOTES

Hole in the Sky:

[1] Sound of the deep-timbred drum associated with Earthdance
[2] Literally: The-world-abhors-the-truth. Yoruba name for parrot; 'radio of the forest'
[3] Highly priced tree in the Nigerian rainforest; famous for its majestic height and durability.

Igi Da:

Iroko is regarded as the king of the Nigerian rain forest; *Oganwo* is next in rank; *Omo* is the carpenter's favourite wood for making house doors and windows
In Ikere-Ekiti dialect of Yoruba, *Okere* is male squirrel; *Oyunkun* is the female; *Alagiriwowo* is a squirrel-like rodent that lives in the crevices in the roots of the tall trees; *Akokoligi* is the woodpecker.

Climate of Fear:

An island in South Australia famous for its beauty and abundant nature reserves. It was one of the causalities of the Australia fires of 2019/2020.
A town in California, destroyed by wild fires in 2018.

Malingering Mountain?:

Alapandagi, aro, shawa are kinds of fishes in the tropical waters of Nigeria.

Dying Lake:

A friend's remark after a visit to Lake Chad

Kaningo:

An important river in Freetown, Sierra Leone; major inspiration for *Sacred River*, Syl Cheney Coker's epic novel.
Said Cheney Coker, ruefully, as he pointed at the Kaningo during our visit to Freetown in May 2016 for the shooting of the documentary, *The Poets*.

Venice Under Water:

Water has invaded the homestead
The street is besieged by floods

Head in the Sand:

He deceives himself
Oh he deceives himself
He who tries to gather the rain in a sieve
He is deceiving himself

Remembering Ken Saro Wiwa:

A renowned Nigerian writer and environmentalist hanged in 1995 by Nigeria's military junta for his environmental activism. He was once President of the Association of Nigerian Authors (ANA).

For Greta Thunberg:

Swedish teenager who has touched the conscience of the world with her environmental/climate activism.
[1] A Yoruba saying: When elders lack the wisdom that comes with age/ Children will rise up to mend the lack.
[2] Also known as Women for Life on Earth

The Delta Sings Between the Tides:

Direct references to J.P. Clark's *A Reed in the Tide*; Gabriel Okara's "River Nun – III"; Tanure Ojaide's "In the Omoja River"; Ogaga Ifowodo's *The Oil Lamp*; Ibiwari Ikiriko's *Oily Tears*; Nnimmo Bassey's *We Thought It Was Oil But It Was Blood*.

For Ibiwari Ikiriko:

Late Nigerian poet and academic; author of *Oily Tears of The Delta*.

Invocation:

Composed and performed for Guardians of the Flame community at the opening ceremony of Mardi Gras 2010 in New Orleans.

Many Stars, One Sky:

A Yoruba phrase that usually introduces a riddle

For World Food Day:

World Food Day is celebrated every year across the world on October 16

Oba L'Agbe:

The Farmer is King.
Title of a novel by Jacques Roumain, famous Haitian writer and social activist.

Song of Life (2):

A variety of peppers with varying degrees of spiciness.

Ode to the Pine Apple:
The Yoruba word for pine apple is Ope Oyinbo (the white man's palm).

My Kitchen Is a Garden:

A trans-lingual pun. Literally, 'greet-them-greet-them'; sociable, pleasant

Spirit of Spring:

Excerpt from a personal letter to the author by Mary Jay, former Director of the Oxford, UK-based African Books Collective (ABC).

A Paddle Made of Words:
The New Yorker, March 31, 2008, p.84

Gbarijo:
Literally, gather the heads together

NIYI OSUNDARE

Widely regarded as one of Africa's most renowned poets, scholars, and public intellectuals, Niyi Osundare has authored over 18 books of poetry, two books of selected poems, (with individual poems in over 70 journals and magazines across the world), four plays, a book of essays, and numerous monographs and articles on literature, language, culture, and society. He regards his calling as a writer and his profession as a teacher as essentially complementary. He was educated on three continents: B.A. (Honours) from the University of Ibadan, Nigeria, M.A. from the University of Leeds in England, and Ph.D. from York University, Toronto, Canada.

For his creative works, Osundare has received many prizes and awards, including the ASSOCIATION OF NIGERIAN AUTHORS (ANA) PRIZE, the CADBURY/ANA PRIZE (which he won on two different occasions, 1989 and 1994), the COMMONWEALTH POETRY PRIZE, the NOMA AWARD (Africa's most prestigious book award), the TCHICAYA U TAM'SI AWARD FOR AFRICAN POETRY, (generally regarded as Africa's highest poetry award and the FONLON/NICHOLS AWARD for "excellence in literary creativity combined with significant contributions to Human Rights in Africa". In 2004, his award-winning book of poems, *The Eye of the Earth*, was selected as One of Nigeria's Best 25 Books of the 20th Century by a Jury appointed by Spectrum Books, Nigeria. His poem, "Raindrum" (along with its Yoruba translation) was selected as part of Nigeria's contribution to the cultural events which complemented the 2012 London Olympics. His widely anthologized poem, "I Sing of Change", has been displayed for many weeks on the London Underground and displayed in over 2,000 other spaces around the world. In 2014 he was admitted to the Nigerian National Order of Merit (NNOM), Nigeria's highest recognition for distinguished academic and creative achievement. A strong believer in poetry-as-performance, he has carried out readings and performances of his works in many parts of the world, and his poems have been translated into French, Italian, Slovenian, Korean, German, Dutch, Spanish, Portuguese, Japanese, Arabic, and Serbian. In 2016, he was awarded the Doctor of Letters (D.Litt.) honoris causa, by his alma mater, the University of Ibadan, Nigeria. He has also been a recipient of honorary doctorates from the University of Toulouse in France, and Franklin Pierce University in Rindge New Hampshire, USA. He was a columnist for *Newswatch*, a prominent Nigerian news magazine, from 1986 to 2011. From 1985 to 2003, he ran a weekly poetry column named *Songs of the Season*, in the *Sunday Tribune*, changed the column's name to *Lifelines* the following year, and transferred it to *The Nation* , another leading Nigerian newspaper, in 2007. He is also is a frequent media commentator on social, political, cultural, and literary matters.

In 2015 the NIYI OSUNDARE INTERNATIONAL POETRY FESTIVAL (NOIPOFEST) was inaugurated as an annual festival of poetry readings/performances, scholarly conferences, literary/cultural outreach, and mentoring.

A year later, he featured as one of two African writers (the other being Syl Cheney Coker, the eminent Sierra Leonean poet and novelist) selected by the American organization, DIALOGUETALK (www.dialoguetalk.org) for a major feature documentary entitled *The Poets*, whose filming took place in Sierra Leone (Coker) and Nigeria (Osundare).

At the centre of Osundare's social and literary activism are issues such as Human Rights, social justice, the environment, climate change, and the plight of our Planet. He is Emeritus Distinguished Professor of English at the University of New Orleans, USA, and Visiting Professor at the University of Ibadan, Nigeria.

BLACK WIDOW PRESS MODERN POETS

All the Good Hiding Places by Ralph Adamo

ABC of Translation by Willis Barnstone

The Secret Brain: Selected Poems 1995-2012 by Dave Brinks

Caveat Onus: The Complete Poem Cycle by Dave Brinks

Forgiven Submarine by Andrei Codrescu and Ruxandra Cesereanu

Crusader Woman by Ruxandra Cesereanu

Anticline by Clayton Eshleman

Archaic Design by Clayton Eshleman

Alchemist with One Eye on Fire by Clayton Eshleman

The Price of Experience by Clayton Eshleman

Pollen Aria by Clayton Eshleman

The Essential Poetry (1960 to 2015) by Clayton Eshleman

Grindstone of Rapport: A Clayton Eshleman Reader by Clayton Eshelman

Penetralia by Clayton Eshleman

Clayton Eshleman: The Whole Art Edited by Stuart Kendall

Barzakh (Poems 2000-2012) by Pierre Joris

Packing Light: New & Selected Poems by Marilyn Kallet

How Our Bodies Learned by Marilyn Kallet

The Love That Moves Me by Marilyn Kallet

The Hexagon by Robert Kelly

Fire Exit by Robert Kelly

Garage Elegies by Stephen Kessler

Last Call by Stephen Kessler

Memory Wing by Bill Lavender

from stone this running by Heller Levinson

Un by Heller Levinson

Wrack Lariat by Heller Levinson

LinguaQuake by Heller Levinson

tenebraed by Heller Levinson

SEEP by Heller Levinson

LURK by Heller Levinson

Dada Budapest by John Olson

Backscatter by John Olson

Larynx Galaxy by John Olson

Weave of the Dream King by John Olson

City Without People: The Katrina Poems by Niyi Osundare

An American Unconscious by Mebane Robertson

Signal from Draco: New & Selected Poems by Mebane Robertson

President of Desolation & Other Poems by Jerome Rothenberg

Barbaric Vast & Wild: An Assemblage of Outside & Subterranean Poetry from Origins to Present. Edited by Jerome Rothenberg and John Bloomberg-Rissman

Concealments and Caprichos by Jerome Rothenberg

Eye of Witness: A Jerome Rothenberg Reader. Edited by Heriberto Yepez and Jerome Rothenberg

Soraya by Anis Shivani

Fractal Song by Jerry W. Ward, Jr.

Beginnings Of the Prose Poem—All Over the Place Edited by Mary Ann Caws and Michel Delville

BLACK WIDOW PRESS POETRY IN TRANSLATION

The Great Madness by Avigdor Hameiri. Translated and edited by Peter C. Appelbaum.

Of Human Carnage - Odessa 1918-1920 by Avigdor Hameiri.
Translated and edited by Peter C. Appelbaum. Introduction by Dan Hecht

Howls & Growls: French Poems to Bark By
Translated by Norman R. Shapiro & Illustrated by Olga Pastuchiv

A Flea the Size of Paris: the Old French "Fatrasies" and "Fatras"
Translated by Ted Byrne and Donato Mancini

In Praise of Sleep: Selected Poems of Lucian Blaga by Lucian Blaga.
Translated by Andrei Codrescu

RhymAmusings by Pierre Coran. Translated by Norman R. Shapiro

Through Naked Branches: Selected Poems of Tarjei Vesaas by Tarjei Vesaas.
Translated by Roger Greenwald

I Have Invented Nothing: Selected Poems by Jean-Pierre Rosnay. Translated by J. Kates

Fables of Town & Country by Pierre Coran. Translated by Norman R. Shapiro
& Illustrated by Olga Pastuchiv

Earthlight (Clair de terre): Poems by André Breton. Translated by Bill Zavatsky and Zack Rogow

The Gentle Genius of Cecile Perin: Selected Poems (1906-1956) by Cecile Perin.
Translated by Norman R. Shapiro

Boris Vian Invents Boris Vian: A Boris Vian reader. Edited and Translated by Julia Older
with a Preface by Patrick Vian

Forbidden Pleasures: New Selected Poems [1924-1949] by Luis Cernuda.
Translated by Stephen Kessler

Fables In a Modern Key (Fables Dans L'Air Du Temps) by Pierre Coran.
Translated by Norman R. Shapiro & Illustrated by Olga Pastuchiv

Exile Is My Trade: A Habib Tengour Reader by Habib Tengour. Translated by Pierre Joris

Present Tense of The World: Poems 2000-2009 by Amina Said. Translated by Marilyn Hacker

Endure: Poems by Bei Dao. Translated by Clayton Eshleman and Lucas Klein

Curdled Skulls: Poems of Bernard Bador by Bernard Bador.
Co-translated and edited by Clayton Eshleman

Pierre Reverdy: Poems Early to Late by Pierre Reverdy.
Translated by Mary Ann Caws and Patricia Terry

Selected Prose and Poetry of Jules Supervielle by Jules Supervielle.
Translated by Nancy Kline, Patrica Terry, and Kathleen Micklow

Poems of Consummation by Vicente Aleixandre. Translated by Stephen Kessler

A Life of Poems, Poems of a Life by Anna de Noailles. Translated by Norman R. Shapiro

Furor & Mystery and Other Poems by Rene Char. Translated by Mary Ann Caws and Nancy Kline

The Big Game (Le grand jeu) by Benjamin Péret. Translated by Marilyn Kallet

Essential Poems & Prose of Jules Laforgue by Jules Laforgue. Translated by Patricia Terry

Preversities: A Jacques Prevert Sampler by Jacques Prevert. Translated by Norman R. Shapiro

La Fontaine's Bawdy by Jean de la Fontaine. Translated by Norman R. Shapiro
& Illustrated by David Schorr

Inventor of Love by Gherasim Luca. Translated by Julian and Laura Semilian

Art Poetique by Guillevic. Translated by Maureen Smith with Lucie Albertini Guillevic

To Speak, to Tell You? by Sabine Sicaud. Translated by Norman R. Shapiro

Poems of A. O. Barnabooth by Valery Larbaud. Translated by Ron Padgett and Bill Zavatsky

EyeSeas (Les Ziaux) by Raymond Queneau. Translated by Daniela Hurezanu and Stephen Kessler

Essential Poems and Writings of Joyce Mansour by Joyce Mansour. Translated by Serge Gavronsky

Essential Poems and Writings of Robert Desnos: A Bilingual Anthology by Robert Desnos. Translated by Mary Ann Caws, Terry Hale, Bill Zavatsky, Martin Sorrell, Jonathan Eburne, Katherine Connelly, Patricia Terry, and Paul Auster

The Sea and Other Poems (1977-1997) by Guillevic. Translated by Patricia Terry

Love, poetry, (L'Amour La Poesie, 1929) by Paul Eluard. Translated by Stuart Kendall

Capital of Pain by Paul Eluard. Translated by Mary Ann Caws, Patricia Terry, and Nancy Kline

Poems of André Breton, A Bilingual Anthology. Translated by Jean-Pierre Cauvin and Mary Ann Caws

Last Love Poems of Paul Eluard Translated by Marilyn Kallet

Approximate Man' & Other Writings by Tristan Tzara. Translated by Mary Ann Caws

Chanson Dada: Selected Poems of Tristan Tzara. Translated by Lee Harwood

Disenchanted City: La ville désenchantée by Chantel Bizzini. Translated by Marilyn Kallet and J. Bradford Anderson

Guarding the Air: Selected Poems of Gunnar Harding. Translated by Roger Greenwald

BLACK WIDOW PRESS BIOGRAPHY

Revolution of the Mind: The Life of Andre Breton by Mark Polizzotti